# THE WESTERN LITURGY
# AND ITS HISTORY

*Some Reflections on Recent Studies*

BY

## THEODOR KLAUSER

*Professor of Church History in the University of Bonn*

TRANSLATED INTO ENGLISH

BY

## F. L. CROSS

*Lady Margaret Professor of Divinity in the University of Oxford
and Canon of Christ Church*

## LONDON
A. R. MOWBRAY & Co. LIMITED
NEW YORK : MOREHOUSE-GORHAM CO.

First published, 1952

PRINTED IN GREAT BRITAIN BY
A. R. MOWBRAY & CO. LIMITED IN THE CITY OF OXFORD
2152

# TRANSLATOR'S PREFACE

IN a collection of his *opuscula*, which the author of the following pages was kind enough to send me a short time ago, he included a paper with the title *Abendländische Liturgiegeschichte*. As soon as I began to read it, I felt that it was a survey for which many English-speaking students, and perhaps others too, were looking. If our Eucharistic worship is to be intelligent we Christians in Great Britain as almost all children of the Western Liturgy should know at least something of its long and tangled history and of the influences under which it has taken shape. But many English Churchmen have long been at a disadvantage. For though awareness of the practical aspects of the subject may have increased in the last decade, notably through the influence of Dom Gregory Dix's stimulating and invaluable study on *The Shape of the Liturgy*, and our younger students may be slowly becoming conscious of the lively interest in the origins of the Western Liturgy which has grown up on the Continent in the last fifty years and of the radical reconstruction which this has required in the doctrines of Duchesne and his contemporaries, many of these researches are contained in periodicals and works which can be readily studied only by the scholar with access to large libraries. A great merit of Dr. Klauser's essay is that it gives a lucid and comprehensive survey of these discoveries in a form wholly free from technicalities and without ever losing sight of their practical implications. I have little doubt that the following pages will be warmly welcomed not only by those with the historical interests of the student but also by many others who, with no pretensions to being professional liturgists, week by week, or day by day, find in the Eucharistic Liturgy the centre of their worship.

Professor Theodor Klauser will need no introduction to professed students of liturgy, who have long recognized in him one of the chief German authorities in the field. It should only be added that he is closely associated with the many in German-speaking countries, and indeed throughout Europe, who are thinking constructively about the liturgy and alive to the possibilities of constructive reform, and that his very high academic distinction and rank—he has recently been Rector of the University of Bonn—give his judgements enhanced authority in a field where readiness to express opinion is not always accompanied by solid learning or liturgical sense.

It may be added that the following pages were written in 1943 for circulation among students on active service and reissued in the following year in a very modest format in *Eleutheria*, Bonner theologische Blätter für kriegsgefangene Studenten, Heft 1 (1944). In the intervening years progress in liturgical studies has continued. Not only has the interest in liturgy deepened, but some historical work of the first importance has been carried out. There seems little doubt that the recent studies in the interrelation of the

Roman Sacramentaries which we owe to such scholars as Dom Bernard Capelle, Mgr. C. Callewaert, Dr. A. Stuiber and Professor A. Chavasse, are a permanent and most important contribution to the history of the Proper, perhaps the most characteristic element in the Western Liturgy. At a different level the massive *Missarum Sollemnia* of the Austrian Jesuit, Joseph Andreas Jungmann (who is mentioned at more than one point in these pages), has put into the hands of the student an invaluable tool for carrying his studies further.

It only remains to thank Professor Klauser for his great generosity in allowing this paper to appear in England. For the convenience of students I have added a bibliography of the principal publications referred to in the text and also a list of some of Professor Klauser's own papers.

F. L. CROSS

CHRIST CHURCH, OXFORD
*8 May 1952*

# CONTENTS

# THE WESTERN LITURGY AND ITS HISTORY

## INTRODUCTION

Our ancient cathedral churches, which were designed as buildings with well-defined outlines in the Norman or Gothic style, have long since become in many ways confusing structures. Every century has left traces of its own devotional forms and spiritual and aesthetic interests. Round the choir and aisles a ring of chapels of various patterns has been added. The walls have gradually been covered with monuments to the dead. The framework of the windows has been repeatedly altered and filled with painted glass of widely different dates. Statues and tombs, lights and lecterns, Sacrament houses and stalls everywhere break up the flowing and graceful lines of the body of the church. And by reason of the number and richness of their successors, the few altars of long ago no longer stand out in prominence. To-day it is only the few trained students who can survey the whole and grasp its spiritual meaning, while the fruits of their varied investigations are of such gigantic dimensions that they almost fill to overflowing the hidden recesses of the large volumes of the officially sponsored inventories.

Not dissimilar, though much more complex, is the

confusion in the Roman Liturgy of the West in its present state. Here the history covers not a single millennium, but almost two. In deep and ineffaceable characters it bears the marks of the spiritual development not of a single people, but of several. The most diverse influences, assuming ever new forms, have played their part in fashioning the structure and composition of our liturgy. They include the sober but majestic masculine temper of the early Christian Popes; the zealous devotion of the early monasteries, with its wholehearted attachment to the *opus dei* and carelessness of its claims on time; the enthusiastic delight of the clerics of the Merovingian and Carolingian eras in the use of symbols; the deeply emotional experience of the medieval mystics and, contemporaneous with it, the analytic intellect of the Scholastics; later, the love of ornament in the Baroque period; and lastly (and yet going very deep) the unhistorical attachment to legality of the rubricists of modern times. Who can hope to be sufficient to survey, to expound and to interpret the final result of this long process of transformation with its many and closely interpenetrating lines of development?

But in spite of all this the Liturgy must be understood. For day by day it is our duty to live in it and from it. At the least we must have such knowledge of the decisive turning points in its history as will furnish us with an ever-ready key to the rudimentary understanding of its several elements.

The purpose of the following pages will be to survey and describe these transformations in the liturgy, as they appear to a student of the subject at the present time. They will divide the history of the Western Liturgy into four periods. The first will take us down to Gregory the Great, i.e. to 590; the second to Gregory VII, i.e. to 1073; the third to the Council of Trent, i.e. to 1545; and finally the fourth down to the present day. Of these four periods, the first may be described as the period of creative beginnings; the second as that of Franco-German leadership; the third as the era of unification; and lastly the fourth as the age of changelessness or of rubricism. In each case a brief survey of the period as it appeared to the older scholars will be given first, to be followed by some account of the principal facts which recent study has brought to light.

# I

# THE EPOCH OF CREATIVE BEGINNINGS

## FROM THE EARLIEST TIMES TO GREGORY THE GREAT

1. A student wishing to describe in brief compass what was known say in 1914 about the earliest period of the Christian liturgy might put the matter somewhat as follows: The fundamental acts of Christian worship —Eucharist, Sacraments and Common Prayer—all go back to the express command of the Lord or at any rate (e.g. Common Prayer) to His commendation. But in so far as the methods by which these religious acts were to be carried out were not expressly laid down by Christ Himself, it was otherwise. These were only to a small extent the creations of the Primitive Christian Church. For the most part they were taken over from the religious practice either of Judaism or of the Hellenistic world.

From Jewish sources came the substance of the Service of the Word which survives in the pre-Mass, i.e. the lections and the accompanying sermon. Both of these were taken over from the morning service of the Sabbath. Of Jewish origin, too, was the essential structure of the ancient Eucharistic prayer preserved in our Canon. It was derived from the Hymn of Praise for Creation and for God's gracious leading of Israel, used in every Sabbath morning service. Of Jewish origin, again, were the essentials of the daily prayers, viz. the morning and evening devotions, the triple number of the day hours, the threefold division of the night prayers, and the reckoning of the liturgical day from evening to evening. Of Jewish origin, finally, were the Doxology, the religious use of the Tersanctus, and the three 'acclamations' *Amen*, *Alleluia*, and *Maranatha*.

By contrast it was rather to the Hellenistic world and its mystery religions (it was argued) that we must certainly turn to discover the decisive influences on the formation of the Christian Baptismal rite with its exorcisms and anointings. From Hellenism, too, came the idea of transferring the Celebration of Baptism to the Easter night. From Hellenism there also came the *disciplina arcani*, i.e. the primitive Christian custom of observing silence about what lay at the centre of its religious acts. From Hellenism again came the tendency to make the formulae of prayer conform with the laws of ancient rhetoric, especially the law of symmetry. From Hellenism, once again, came innumerable liturgical technical terms, among them the word *liturgy* itself as well as such words as *mystery*, *anaphora*, *canon*, *preface* and *anamnesis*. Lastly from the same source came certain forms of prayer, including those of the type of the Litany of the Saints and the acclamations *Kyrie eleison*, *Dignum et justum est*, etc.

To put the matter concretely, what happened was something like this. In drawing on these two sources, Jewish and Hellenistic, and in adding thereto from its own resources, the early Christian liturgy underwent some such development as follows. At the outset, there were two forms of Divine service, the Service of the Word, held on Sunday mornings, with its lections, sermon and prayer, and the liturgical meal on Sunday evenings, consisting of the Celebration of the Eucharist in conjunction with a full meal which was either introduced by the Eucharist or more probably formed the framework of the Eucharist proper. At an early date the meal was separated under the name of the Agape, presumably in view of the growing size of the congregations and the consequent increase in technical and disciplinary difficulties; and in the course of the fourth century it died out altogether. The Celebration of the Eucharist, on the other hand, was removed, probably in the second century, to the morning, and combined with the Service of the Word. In very early times the faithful used to bring to the single evening meal gifts of all kinds. After the separation of the Eucharist and the Agape they continued to bring their gifts to both religious meals. In this custom, combined with the regular practice in the ancient world for members of the community themselves to present their sacrificial offerings, lie the roots of the so-called Offertory Procession. The Eucharistic prayers were at first freely improvised by the Bishop, who followed a traditional pattern; at the next stage, previous preparation of the prayer at home became customary; finally the use of set texts composed by someone else became the rule. The recognized language of the liturgy in the first centuries, at Rome as elsewhere, was Greek. At Rome the transition to the use of Latin took place about the middle of the third century: for it was at roughly this date that the Greek tongue began to disappear from the civic life of the Imperial capital. To the original feast of Easter, with its extension over the ensuing fifty days and its weekly repetition on Sundays, further liturgical commemorations were added in the fourth century, among them Christmas and Epiphany and the first feasts of the Martyrs. The elaboration of this basic structure to a religious ordering of the whole year from Advent to Pentecost was completed in essentials by the end of the sixth century. From the beginning of the fourth century the daily hours of prayer, which had originally been observed only in private, became established in the monastic houses as a communal observance. In the course of the fourth century this common form of the hours also became a regular practice in the rest of the Church.

Such, in general terms, was the picture which students round about 1914 drew of the primitive Christian liturgy. The remarkable intensity with which studies in this field have been pursued in recent years enables us to make it more precise and to amplify it at certain points.

2. Until the First World War the so-called Leonine Sacramentary, a private collection of Mass prayers which, written over a considerable period of time by individual Popes and preserved in the Papal archives, was finished *c.* 530, was held to be the oldest Roman liturgical book. But in 1916 the English Benedictine scholar, Dom Hugh Connolly, conclusively established the thesis, already adumbrated by Eduard Schwartz,

that the document hitherto known as the 'Egyptian Church Order' embodied a still older book from the City of Rome than the Sacramentary just mentioned and that this book, indeed, was none other than the manual which Hippolytus, the Roman Anti-Pope and later Martyr, compiled *c.* 220 under the title of the *Apostolic Tradition.*

The significance of this discovery can hardly be overestimated. With a single stroke we have reached a fixed point in the early history of the Roman liturgy. Indeed, by this discovery the liturgy of the Age of the Martyrs has been made directly accessible. The objection might be raised that perhaps Hippolytus, the head of a schismatic community, did not incorporate in his book the traditional practices of Rome, but gave us a wholly new Order drawn up by himself. But this objection overlooks the fact that in his struggle with Pope Callistus, Hippolytus was pre-eminently the upholder of tradition, the ardent spokesman of conservative circles in Rome. Moreover, the fact that Hippolytus' treatise was in use over several centuries in the most widely separated provinces of the Church, in the East as well as in the West, is proof that it was considered a wholly orthodox body of liturgical regulations and one consonant with tradition. We may even conclude from the extensive use made of it over several centuries that it met a deeply felt need. It seems probable that Hippolytus' work was the first book to provide liturgical formulae which were directly adapted for practical use and that therewith a decisive turning-point in the history of the liturgy was reached. The age of charismatic leadership and local multiplicity was coming to its end and the era of statutory liturgical regulation and growing uniformity beginning.

Hippolytus' book treats of the Ordination forms for the higher and lower clergy, for widows and virgins; further, of the Catechumenate and Baptism; lastly, of fasting, agapes and the hours. The Baptismal rite outlined by Hippolytus already contains the exorcisms and anointings which are still in use to-day. On the other hand the present form of the Trinitarian Baptismal formula is as yet unknown. By contrast, Baptism is given in relation to the three parts of the Credal confession, arranged in the interrogatory form. This interrogatory form will have lain close at hand through the usages of Roman contractual law. Infant Baptism is already the established practice. The Eucharistic prayer, which is given in the context of the Consecration Form for a Bishop, already shows the basic outline of our canon, though the Sanctus is wanting. Hans Lietzmann, the well-known Berlin theologian (d. 1942), deduced from an analysis of this text that it must be an elaboration, in the direct line of development, of the Eucharistic prayer which was current in the communities founded by St. Paul.

I must leave the reader to consider and think out the significance for his personal participation in the liturgy of this observation on the development, now extending over 1,900 years, of the Eucharistic prayer. He may be referred, however, to Anton Baumstark's fine observations on 'supra-temporal community-consciousness' (*überzeitlichen Gemeinschaftsbewusstsein*) at the outset of his little book *Vom geschichtlichen Werden der Liturgie* (1923).

3. At the time of Hippolytus, as his texts show, the language of the Roman liturgy was still Greek. This fact is not at all surprising. The very great majority of the population of Rome, who to a large extent had come from the East and, as far as its upper strata were concerned, were dominated by Greek culture, spoke Greek down to about the middle of the third century. A hundred and fifty years after Hippolytus a Roman writer, Marius Victorinus, cited a fragment of the Roman Canon in a Latin writing. As Victorinus here passes over, without comment, to the Greek language, we have a sure token that at that date at least the Canon, if not indeed all the Mass prayers, was recited in Greek. Twenty years later another Roman writer cited another fragment of the Canon, but now in Latin. If we further observe that close points of contact exist between the language of the Latin Canon and the style and expressions of certain Roman writers of the end of the fourth century, we may assert with some certainty that it was found about 380, i.e. under Pope Damasus (366–384), that the Latin language made its entry into the Roman Mass, or, more precisely, into its most important part.

Was the Latin Canon which then came into being something completely new? Or did it arise from the translation of a Greek original? Some years ago Anton Baumstark endeavoured to defend the latter thesis. He argued that the phrase in the Canon, *summus sacerdos tuus Melchisedech*, 'Thy most high priest, Melchisedek', owed its striking form, which differs from that in the Bible, to an error of translation. To be more precise, he held that when the Greek Canon was put into Latin, the translator, foundering on the difficulties of the Greek form of words, made of a 'Priest of God Most High' a 'Most High Priest of God'. But however ingenious and compelling Baumstark's argumentation may appear, it cannot stand up to a more radical testing. For even if we suppose that an error of translation underlies the phrase in the Canon, must it have been none other than the author of the Canon who made the mistake? May not the writer of the Canon have taken the expression from an already extant text, namely the Latin Bible? And, apart from this possibility, Dom Bernard Botte has been able to show that *c.* 380 Melchisedek was already termed 'High Priest' (ἀρχιερεύς) also in the Greek-speaking East. Hence the Latin rendering in question certainly need not have arisen from an erroneous translation. It probably corresponds to a designation, already generally current, of the Old Testament Priest-King.

But on the other hand the Latin Canon was certainly not something wholly new. In the course of the centuries a fixed pattern for the Eucharistia, the great Prayer of Thanksgiving, had crystallized out, a pattern which was everywhere followed in East and West alike. It was the universal practice to incorporate into the Eucharistia the Institution Narrative, as well as an Epiclesis (i.e. a prayer for the consecratory intervention of the Holy Ghost), an Anamnesis (i.e. a prayer recalling the Passion, Resurrection and Ascension of the Lord), a prayer for the acceptance of the sacrificial gifts and lastly intercession for the living and the dead. Together with these elements of thanksgiving there were also certain formulae and expressions which became the common property of churches almost everywhere. It was an accepted rule that one began with the dialogue 'Lift up your hearts', that the transition from the Institution Narrative to the Anamnesis was made with the expression 'Wherefore mindful', that the angels surrounding the altar were mentioned, that the Eucharistic Gifts were described as a 'spiritual (pneumatic) sacrifice' and that the commemoration of the living and the dead was introduced by the formula 'Remember, Lord'. Hence we may sum up by saying: When the transition was made from Greek to Latin and the text was given a new form, the traditional stream of thought was preserved, while certain expressions, drawn from the spirit of the Latin language, which had been consecrated by previous usage, were adopted. Such an account of what happened would sufficiently explain the similarities which we have already noticed between the canon of Hippolytus and our own.

In this connexion, Odo Casel, the well-known Benedictine scholar of Maria Laach, made the very significant observation that the noteworthy description of the Eucharistic Sacrifice as *'oblatio rationabilis'*, i.e. as a 'pneumatic, spiritual sacrifice', which is already met with in the Roman Canon of the fourth century, finds its only linguistic parallel in St. Ambrose of Milan. This important observation forms the basis of the conjecture, which receives additional support from other considerations, that the Latin canon which came into being in the fourth century and is still in use to-day was the creation not of a Bishop of Rome but of the great restorer of the Milanese Liturgy. From this it would follow that the transition from Greek to Latin as the language of the liturgy was first carried through, not at Rome but at Milan. Ambrose (374–397), and not Damasus, would have to be accounted the pioneer of the Latin Liturgy, though to Damasus we should still owe a great debt for having secured general recognition for the bold step of the Bishop of Milan by giving it the authoritative support of the Roman See.

When we reflect that the Latin language began to predominate in the leading cities of Italy at latest *c.* 250, i.e. roughly at the date at which the Popes began to set Latin inscriptions on the tombs of their predecessors, we must infer that for at least 120 years the language of the liturgy in the West was at variance with that of the people. In this way had already come into being the cleft between the language of the liturgy and the vernacular, which many nowadays reckon a tragedy, though others regard it as a providential disposition in that by the distinctive language of the liturgy its character as a mystery is the more strongly emphasized. It is in the highest degree instructive for us to observe, however, that the early Church tolerated this cleft only as a passing phenomenon. It abandoned Greek, which had been the language of religious worship in the Apostolic Age and the Age of the Martyrs, without reservation in favour of the vernacular. As the contemporary observations of Ambrosiaster (PL. 17.209) clearly show, the Church was conscious that in so doing it was acting along the lines laid down by St. Paul. St. Paul had made it a rule, primarily in reference to the appearance of charismatics in the community, that liturgical prayer should be intelligible to the congregation on the ground that the congregation should make it its own, something it could only do if it were to assent to it with its 'Amen', and also that it should be able to derive edification from it. *I will pray with the spirit, and I will pray with the understanding also. . . . Else when thou shalt bless with the spirit, how shall he that occupieth the room of the unlearned say Amen at thy giving of thanks, seeing he understandeth not what thou sayest? For thou verily givest thanks well, but the other is not edified* (1 *Cor.* xiv. 15–17). At a time when men's minds are constantly turning to the question of putting the liturgy into the vernacular (*Verdeutschung der Liturgie*), these facts should never be lost sight of. We are only following the pattern of the liturgy in its classical age if we defend the principle that it should also in some measure be intelligible to the simple man, and particularly, of course, those parts of it which convey instruction.

4. The liturgical Greek of Hippolytus, and still more the Latin of the Leonine Sacramentary and of the other collections, teems with expressions familiar

to the philologist from the language of ancient worship and especially of the mystery religions. We refer here to such words as *mysterium, actio, memoria, illuminatio, invocatio* and their Greek equivalents. We are thus led to inquire whether these expressions, when taken over into the Christian liturgy, retained the concrete context which was associated with them in ancient worship, or, on the other hand, whether at the moment when they were adopted by the Church the words were given a new, perhaps an abstractly spiritual, significance. Or, to make the problem clear by an example, did the word *mysterium* in these primitive liturgical formulae mean 'a secret' or did it still retain its classical meaning of a 'holy dedicatory action'?

Odo Casel, who examined this question in innumerable, mainly philological, studies, was led to hold that the expressions in question continued to retain their traditional meaning in the framework of the Christian liturgy. On the basis of these philological investigations he concluded that the creator of the Roman liturgy recognized in the Celebration of the Eucharist and of the Sacraments sacred mystery-actions (*heilige Mysterienhandlungen*) in the sense characteristic of antiquity, i.e. actions which beneath a symbolical husk enabled the fact of the Redeemer's mystical but real Presence to be given historical actuality. That this conception was no mere passing stream of opinion in the third and fourth centuries but the universal conviction of the Church from the time of St. Paul down to the classical age of Scholasticism (*Hochscholastik*),

Casel sought to establish by a thorough testing of the tradition.

Scholars have not as yet given unqualified assent to Casel's conclusions. In particular his opponents have pointed out that he has so far[1] given no satisfactory theoretical, i.e. reasoned, explanation of the so-called Mystery-Doctrine (*Mysterienlehre*). On the other hand it must be recognized that what we are here primarily concerned with is not the speculative problems bound up with the Mystery-Doctrine (in the meantime Gottlieb Söhngen in particular has devoted attention to these), but a historical question which must ultimately be resolved by philological methods, namely whether the early Church had this conception of the Mass and Sacraments or not. As regards this question, I believe the real facts to be that in certain definite, namely Eastern, parts of the Church and for individual Fathers the Mystery-Conception is capable of proof, but that the other parts of the Church, and notably the neighbourhood of Rome, can be shown to have been only occasionally affected by it. Hence it would appear that the Mystery-Doctrine of the Liturgy was the source of only one theological interpretation of the rite (though of one which was, indeed, introduced by a St. Paul), and that owing to the accession to the Church of many who had grown up in the Pagan mystery-cults this interpretation won many disciples at certain times and in certain regions; but that it never became the universally accepted possession of the

---

[1] This, of course, was written before Casel's death during the night of Holy Saturday, 1948. [F.L.C.]

Church. Nevertheless, in spite of this critique of Casel's results, we must gratefully recognize that he has restored to many words, phrases and ceremonies in the liturgy their primitive rich significance, that he has offered us a new and more organic understanding of the Sacramental rites and that beyond this he has exercised a stimulating and provocative influence on Theology.

5. Another fruitful influence has been exerted by the studies initiated by Joseph Andreas Jungmann on the Place of the Christ in Liturgical Prayer. It had long been observed that the Eucharistic prayers of the primitive liturgy were directed almost exclusively to the Father and that Christ was allowed to take His place in them only as the Mediator (*Deus qui . . ., per Dominum nostrum . . .*), whereas the forms of prayer dating from the Middle Ages and more recent times for the most part address Christ Himself. But hitherto it had not been known when and through what circumstances the change was brought about. On the basis of a careful comparison of all the relevant liturgical texts Jungmann proved conclusively that the impulse to the change came from the Arian struggles of the fourth century. These struggles gradually led to increased emphasis on the Godhead of Christ and thus brought about a weakening of the conception, so strongly stressed by the Lord Himself and also by St. Paul, of the High Priestly Mediatorial Office of Christ. None the less, this last undoubtedly remains one of the basic pillars of Christian thought and is ever therefore in need of revived cultivation.

6. There is but little that recent investigation can tell us about the beginnings of the liturgical insignia and the origins of the ceremonial with which the celebration of Solemn High Mass and of the Pontifical Rites is invested. The oldest ritual authorities, the so-called *Ordines*, only take us back to about the second half of the seventh century, and here we find that the development is already far advanced or, indeed, if we consider that in the City of Rome as alone authoritative, by now complete. In these *Ordines* we find no answer to the question when genuflexion before the Pope, when kissing of the foot and hand, when the throne, incense and portable lights made their way into the Liturgy, when the Bishop or the Priest first wore their characteristic vestments and insignia such as the ring, the *pallium*, the *mappula* (maniple) and the stole.

But recently a Hungarian classical historian, Andreas Alföldi, has given us for the first time a connected account of the development of the Monarchical ceremonial at the Roman Imperial Court. We are very surprised to discover the existence of close points of contact between the Roman-Byzantine Court-ceremonial and the rules for the Papal Mass of the seventh century, i.e. the ceremonial which still survives in every Pontifical rite and, to a more limited extent, in every High Mass with deacon and subdeacon. The similarity is so great that, as will emerge from a more detailed study of the connexions of which I made preliminary studies several years ago, it is now certain that the marks of honour and the ceremonial of the Imperial Court and of the highest rank of officials were transferred at some stage to the Bishops and other clerics and thus found entrance into the Liturgy. It is less easy to say precisely how this development came about. But it is certain that it began as soon as the State and the Church entered into alliance. For at that moment the State was obliged to allocate to the Bishops, Priests and Deacons their place in the civil order of rank and grant them the insignia and marks of honour corresponding to the ranks assigned to them. Since the Bishops were put on a level with those holding the highest civil rank, they received the throne, lights, incense, *mappula*, the kissing of the hand and other marks of honour, and since the Bishop of Rome was ranked with the Imperial Majesty himself, he could lay claim, like the Emperor, to the ring, genuflexion, kissing of the foot and the setting up of his portrait in the official chambers, i.e. in the churches. It was for the Church to decide whether and how far within the spiritual realm she would make use of such rights granted to her office-bearers by the State. When in the course of the third century Paul of Samosata, Bishop of Antioch and at the same time the holder of a high civil office, set up in his cathedral 'a podium (*bema*) with a high throne' and in his episcopal lodgings 'an audience chamber as did the secular officials', he aroused great offence among his fellow-Bishops (Euseb. *h.e.* 7.30.9). But when at the beginning of the fourth century such tokens of respect were conceded by the State to the Bishops as a whole, the matter appeared in a new light. It was felt rather that the authority of the ecclesiastical leaders would now be strengthened by surrounding them with the adornment of the civil titles and the civil ceremonial. ·

Recognition of the secular origin of these parts of our liturgy can, indeed, save us from attaching too great an importance to them, especially as we must admit that we sometimes gain the impression that by an over-emphasis on external decoration, the minds of the faithful were diverted from the sublime kernel of the Liturgy to an inordinate degree.

7. Lastly, we must not overlook the fact that the study of the earliest period has also helped us to a more exact understanding of the essential character- istics of the Roman Liturgy. In contrast to modern prayer, the tendency of which is in the main indivi- dualistic and subjective and inclines to a type of thought which is at once abstract and logically pro- gressive, the ancient Liturgy was conditioned by objectivity, preference for the concrete, and a mode of thought which can roughly be described as contem- plative.

All who wish to encourage liturgical prayer and to make it intelligible to themselves and others should be clear about the nature of these distinctive qualities. In this connexion Romano Guardini's classical book, *Vom Geist der Liturgie*,[1] can be of the greatest service.

[1] Eng. tr. as *The Spirit of the Liturgy* (1930). [F.L.C.]

# II

# THE EPOCH OF FRANCO-GERMAN LEADERSHIP

## FROM GREGORY THE GREAT TO GREGORY VII

1. With regard to the second period in the development of the Roman Liturgy, which according to our plan covers the years 590 to 1073, liturgists round about 1914 had only very imperfect and confused ideas. It was the custom to speak of it somewhat as follows: Under Gregory the Great the Roman Liturgy received its final form and found its concrete embodiment in the so-called Gregorian Sacramentary, in the Gregorian Antiphonary and in the so-called Ordines and other collections. In this form, which underwent another final re-shaping at the hands of Pope Hadrian at the end of the eighth century, the Roman Liturgy was naturalized first in England and then under Charlemagne in the Franco-German Empire. In Charlemagne's dominions it came into contact with the remnants of the ancient Gallican liturgy as well as with an older Roman model of it which passed under the name of Pope Gelasius (492–6) and had already crossed the Alps in the sixth or at the beginning of the seventh century. Out of the conflict of these three traditions, the Gallican, the Gelasian and the Gregorianic-Roman, there came into being a mixed product

from which numerous items penetrated to Rome about the year 1000 or soon after.

During this period there was no trace of any real progress in the development of the Roman Liturgy. The liturgical spirit of the time was conditioned above all by the circumstance that the allegorical interpretation of rites and texts which began in France was then entering upon its victorious course. At the same time, in accord with the new type of popular devotion, the Suffering Christ and the Christ present in the Eucharist came increasingly into the foreground of pious consideration.

2. Modern study has put into our hands several facts which indicate that the primary object of Gregory the Great in his final arrangement and ordering of his liturgical inheritance was to abbreviate the parts of the liturgy which had become too long and thus to lighten what had become an excessive burden on the faithful and failed to assist the growth of devotion. Unless I am wholly mistaken, one item in the older Roman Liturgy of the Mass which fell a victim to these shortening endeavours of Gregory (which in my opinion we can rightly regret in this case) was the Intercessory Prayer. In order to explain and justify this assertion, I must develop in brief outline the history of this Intercessory Prayer.

At Rome, as elsewhere, the Service of the Word comprised in the Liturgy concluded with the Dismissal of the Catechumens. At the second part of the Liturgy—including the Offertory Procession, the Consecration and the Communion—only the baptized, the 'fideles', were allowed to be present. But before the Offertory Procession began, the assembled company first prayed for the general needs of the community; and it is this prayer which the sources term the *oratio fidelium*, the 'Prayer of the Faithful'.

In Rome the form of this prayer was invariable. The leader of the Service, making use of a formula which in its basic outlines was always the same, first invited those present to pray with him to God in a definite sense: 'Let us pray, dearly beloved, for the Holy Church of God, that our God and Lord may be pleased to endue it with His grace, peace, unity and protection in all the earth, that He may put in subjection to it the (demonic) principalities and powers, and that He may bestow on us the means of glorifying the Almighty Father in a quiet and untroubled life. Let us pray!' In response to this bidding of the leader of the Liturgy, the congregation gave itself for a space to silent devotion. Then the Celebrant again raised his voice to gather together in a short formula the prayers of all. The congregation, which had raised its arms in the attitude of prayer during the last petition, expressed its assent with a loud 'Amen'. In this way prayer was made in turn for all the concerns of the community, for the Sacred Ministry, for the Confessors, Virgins and Widows, for the Emperor, for Catechumens, for the Sick and the Needy, for Heretics and Schismatics, for Jews and Heathens. When it happened to be a penitential day, the silent prayer was said kneeling and only the concluding prayer standing. The deacon gave the sign for this by calling out: *Flectamus genua*! ('let us kneel down') and *Levate*! ('rise up'). We might almost say that this form of prayer successfully combined the silent devotion of the individual and the audible prayer of the congregation, and thereby mental and bodily dedication in the service of God. But it had one considerable limitation. It was a little circumstantial and, by frequent repetition, could become wearisome.

In the East, and also, under Eastern influence, in Gaul and Upper Italy, another and shorter form of the Intercessory Prayer was current. The Deacon himself announced the subject of intercession in the briefest form of prayer and the congregation completed the prayer with a 'Kyrie eleison!' This is the type of prayer familiar to us under the name of a 'litany'. Its special excellence lies in its combination of brevity, very ready intelligibility and a most living rhythm.

This Eastern form of the Intercessory Prayer commended itself to Pope Gelasius I (492–6). As Dom Bernard Capelle, Abbot of Mont César, has ingeniously proved, Gelasius translated it into Latin and introduced it into the Roman Mass in place of the older native form of the Intercessory Prayer. It is probable that at the same time the position of the prayer was changed, being moved from its position at the beginning of the Mass of the Faithful to the beginning of the Mass of the Catechumens. It thus also ceased to be a 'Prayer of the Faithful'. Only on two days in the year, both in Holy Week, did Gelasius allow the old arrangement to continue. On the Wednesday in Holy Week and on Good Friday the Eucharistic Service began at once in the ancient manner with the Lections, and not until after these were finished did the Intercession follow in the old Roman form. Incidentally we have here a striking instance of an important law of liturgical development which Anton Baumstark has described as the 'Law of the survival of what is ancient in what is liturgically a season of high value' (*Gesetz von der Erhaltung des Alten in liturgisch hochwertiger Zeit*). But also on the other days of the year, a last but feeble trace of the primitive arrangement continued to survive—in this case, no doubt, without the knowledge or consent of Pope Gelasius—namely, the remarkable 'Oremus' at the beginning of the Mass of the Faithful to which no corresponding prayer is attached.

It was this Gelasian form of the Roman Intercessory Prayer which Gregory the Great modified in his work of abbreviation. He set aside the part of the deacon who introduced the prayers and left standing only a last reminder of the response of the faithful, namely, the *Kyrie eleison*. It was only on Holy Saturday—again in conformity with Baumstark's Law just referred to—that everything remained in essentials as hitherto. Down to the present time the Mass on this day begins with a complete Litany.

As far as the abandonment of the Intercessory Prayer was concerned, people in the age of St. Gregory perhaps consoled themselves by reflecting that enough attention was paid to the needs of the Church in the Canon. But the intercessions in the Eucharistic Prayer are expressed in very general terms. Moreover, in view of the fixity of the Canon, they do not permit of any elastic adjustment to needs which change from day to day. And lastly they do not allow of any direct participation by the congregation. Consequently they were unable in the long run to satisfy what was needed, as later developments clearly showed enough. We need only recall the following facts. In many places it was, and still is, the practice at divine service on Sundays to provide, either before or after the Sermon, an extra-liturgical 'General prayer' composed in the vernacular. In Masses for the Dead, it is the custom in many places to interpolate before the beginning of the Sacrifice special vernacular prayers for the dead who are mentioned by name. Finally in times of stress, specially constructed non-Latin prayers have to be introduced at the conclusion of the Mass to act as bridges, as it were, to the concerns which fill the hearts of the members of the congregation. Here an important task for the future reformer of the Western Liturgy is clearly outlined. The first part of the Mass must again be brought into intimate relation to the anxieties, joys and hopes of the moment, as was the case long ago through the Prayer of Intercession.

3. The investigations of the last thirty years, which have been especially fruitful in the field of the Sacramentaries, also enable us to outline to-day with much greater clearness and precision the wanderings of the Roman Liturgy and the active share taken by Franco-German lands in the next stage of its development. We now know—I could bring forward decisive proofs of this fact—that it was not Charlemagne, but Pepin before him who introduced the Gregorian Liturgy of

Rome into his Empire and made it obligatory by royal decree, and that he did this on the occasion of his Coronation in the presence of the Pope in the year 754. This step, which was intended to put an end to the existing liturgical variations and to the competition which had gone on for over a hundred years between the Roman and Gallican Liturgy, met, indeed, with failure at first, owing to technical difficulties. In place of the desired Mass Book which corresponded with the most recent and Gregorian form of the Roman Liturgy, there came into circulation a mixed form in which Gelasian, Gregorian and, to a limited extent, Old Gallican elements were combined into a single unit.

Later Charlemagne once again sought to impose on the Churches of his empire the duty of accepting the pure Gregorian Liturgy and for this purpose deposited authentic Roman books in his Palace Library as patterns for copying. These books, it is true, as I have proved in detail, were very incomplete owing to the carelessness of the Roman authorities. And, what is more, Charlemagne was compelled in the end to recognize that his people were dissatisfied with the pure Roman Liturgy and could not be dissuaded from retaining certain feasts, rites and forms of prayer of long standing. In consequence even before the year 800 an appendix to the Roman Mass Book was compiled, which contained a collection of these native and popular elements and was used side by side with it; but it was to be kept strictly separate from the Roman Mass Book. It is true that the Churches of the Empire

soon turned their backs on this ordinance of Charlemagne. But the fact remains that Charles was success-
ful in making the Gregorian Liturgy the kernel of the
Liturgy of the Empire.

As is well known, chaotic conditions prevailed in
Rome from the end of the ninth century onwards.
The sense for liturgy threatened to die out altogether.
The *scriptoria* for the production of liturgical books
closed down and liturgical life in the Eternal City
would perhaps have come to a complete standstill,
had not some of the monasteries which had been
newly established by the Cluniacs faithfully promoted
it. We must ultimately connect with these circumstances and the expeditions of the Ottos to Rome the
fact that from the end of the tenth century we meet
with texts throughout Italy and above all at Rome
which contain the mixed Romano-Frankish Liturgy.
Or, to put the matter in other words (I am here
repeating what I said many years ago), the Franco-
German Church at a critical juncture saved the Roman
Liturgy for Rome itself and for the world.

4. But that is not all. In the same period the
Franco-German Church also gave to the Roman
Liturgy real enrichment. In recent years the older
view that the structure of the Roman Liturgy was
essentially complete at the end of the sixth century has
been shown to be mistaken. It is true that from the
time of Gregory activity ceased in Rome itself. Just a
few new feasts were fitted into the calendar and, under
Eastern influence, the *Agnus Dei* was incorporated
into the Liturgy of the Mass and the Reproaches

were added to the Good Friday Service. But the impulse to further construction, and above all to an organic development of the post-Pentecostal portion of the Church Year and to a working out of the liturgy of the other Sacraments, was wanting. But it was otherwise in the Franco-German Church. Here in the eighth, ninth and tenth centuries there was great activity, and partly of a creative kind. We used to believe that such things as the solemn anointings in the Ordinations of Clerics, the splendid and symbolical ritual of the Dedication of Churches, the glorious and dramatic Liturgy of Palm Sunday and Holy Week, were derived in essentials from the ancient portions of the Roman Liturgy. This conception has been proved fundamentally wrong. We now know that of the Sacramental rites it is strictly only Baptism which received the greater part of its rich ritual in early Christian Rome. It was the Franco-German Church which, albeit drawing for the purpose on primitive, and in part Eastern, sources, made all the other Sacraments and Sacramentals into what they are to-day. The same is true, as especially Bernard Capelle and Anton Baumstark have shown, of the Liturgy of Palm Sunday and of Holy Week. It is a matter for regret that the gifted liturgists of the Frankish Empire did not also apply themselves to the development of the post-Pentecostal *Proprium de tempore.*

In general, the primitive Roman Liturgy was of almost Puritanical sobriety and brevity. The more pronounced emphasis on the affections, the greater richness in words and symbols, also a certain breadth in action (*Breite der Handlung*), all this—once again with the exception of Baptism—first came into the liturgy through clerics of Germanic, and partly also of Celtic, origin, who worked in the Carolingian Empire. Edmund Bishop once made a very striking comparison of the characteristics of the Old Roman and of the Gallo-Frankish liturgical styles. His classic lecture, *The Genius of the Roman Rite*, especially in its French edition with the comments of André Wilmart, may still be read with the greatest profit.

Finally, as we have been assured by Michel Andrieu, it was clerics from Mainz who round about 950 united the old and new rites to a skilfully ordered collection. Within a short time this collection was supreme in the Western world, including Rome. In our present Pontifical and Ritual the work of these men lives on until the present day.

I need not add how much the knowledge of all these facts can mean for our personal attitude to the Roman Liturgy. *Romana est, sed etiam nostra.*

5. I have indicated in passing that in the seventh and eighth centuries something at least was added to the Liturgy at Rome, too, viz. in the development of the Calendar. First, there was the introduction of the four oldest Feasts of Our Lady, which were all introduced into the Roman Calendar between 609 and 687. Arranged in their order of origin, the list is as follows: The Dedication of the Church S. Maria ad martyres (May 14); the Homegoing of Mary (August 15); Mary's Candlemass (February 2); and Mary's Annunciation (March 25). Apart from the Dedication feast

of May 14, which owed its introduction to local circumstances, they were all taken over from the East, where there is evidence for them at the end of the fifth century. It is also probable that Our Lady's name was first introduced into the Canon of the Roman Mass in the same seventh century.

When we reflect that all these Marian innovations were probably carried through not by native Popes but by the three Syrian Popes of the seventh century, we gain a very clear impression of a further peculiarity of the Roman Liturgy, viz. its tenacious attachment to what is of long standing. Certainly nothing but the existence of an extremely conservative temper can explain the fact that the Roman Liturgy, as contrasted with the practice of the East and of the Gallican West, did not open its doors to the Mother of God until two hundred years after the Council of Ephesus.

# III

# THE EPOCH OF UNIFICATION

## FROM GREGORY VII TO THE COUNCIL OF TRENT

1. As regards the next stage of the Roman Liturgy, which we have agreed to reckon from 1073 to 1545, it was customary thirty years ago to speak somewhat as follows: From Gregory VII onwards the Popes again resumed leadership in the liturgy. It was required of Western sees that they should bind themselves to the liturgical practice ruling at Rome and follow the regulations for the conduct of worship issued by the Pope. But this demand would certainly not have been realized to the full had not the Order of St. Francis of Assisi appeared as an Apostle of the Roman Liturgy in the West. This Order appropriated to itself, at first on grounds of practical convenience, the Missal and the Breviary which were in use in the Pope's private chapel; and through its travelling preachers these convenient Papal books became known throughout the world. In consequence a certain standardization not only of a theoretical and legislative kind, but also in liturgical practice, came about in all lands in the West. A situation was created which later made it possible for the Council of Trent to take in hand the issue of authentic liturgical books of universal obligation.

On the concrete side, notable facts in the liturgical

development of this period were the cessation of Communion under two kinds, the weakening of the understanding of the Eucharistic Sacrifice and of the essential connexion of Sacrifice and Communion, the preference to centre devotion on the Humanity of Christ, and the longing of the growing religious individualism to find increasing satisfaction for its devotional needs outside the Liturgy.

Recent investigation has not led liturgists to require any fundamental changes in this account, but a number of its outlines can now be more clearly drawn. I single out four points.

2. The first concerns the Canon of the Mass. The early Church had naturally left the direction of the action of the liturgy and the performance of the essential consecratory or sacramental acts in the hands of the bishop or the priest as his representative. But it never excluded the participation of the people in the prayers and ceremonial. The people were to be able to follow both alike in every detail and so far from being merely attentive spectators were also to be active participants. The prayers were therefore said aloud. To this the Canon and the Words of Institution were no exception. With a solemn Amen—still retained to-day in the Amen immediately before the Paternoster —the whole congregation gave outward expression to the fact that they had heard and taken part in praying the words of the Canon.

In view of this it is clear that the change to the silent recitation of the sacrificial prayers must be considered a momentous step. Its result was that the bond between priest and people was severed at a crucial point of the Liturgy, that the decisive part of the Celebration became an exclusive concern of the bishop and priest, and that the people were relegated to the rôle of passive spectators. And when once the congregation were excluded from this, why not limit, or even wholly allow to disappear, its often troublesome co-operation which also delayed the course of the action in the non-consecratory portions of the Liturgy? It is evident that here a beginning had been made which was to lead on to the most important consequences. And subsequent history shows that the path which had been entered on was to be pursued to its very end.

But, we may ask, when was that first decisive step taken? A conjecture which lies ready to hand is that it came about at the period when the stream of former members of the ancient Mystery Cults brought with them into the Church a large body of ideas and rites, and when the *disciplina arcani* and the terminology of the Mysteries became accepted in the Church, that is, above all, in the fourth century. But a closer study of the problem has shown that while this conjecture is in the main correct for the East, the more conservative Roman Church, which had less common feeling with the ideas of the Mysteries, held fast to the ancient practice of the audible Canon down to the end of the Patristic period. Only when the Roman Liturgy came into contact with Eastern influences, and this first of all on Gallican soil, was the transition to the silent Canon achieved, i.e. about the seventh century.

Joseph Andreas Jungmann has endeavoured to throw clearer light on this important process, without, however, having reached any decisive conclusions.

3. A second point arising out of recent studies on which I wish to say something concerns the altar. It is a matter of common knowledge that in the early Christian basilicas of Rome, as is still the case to-day, e.g. in the Lateran and S. Clemente, the altar was placed in such a way that the celebrant stood with his face towards the congregation. Moreover, the altar of the early Roman basilica had no shelf for the lights, still less a retable or tabernacle. It was a simple but massive stone table. As is shown by the paintings, e.g. in the lower church of S. Clemente in Rome, which date from the end of the eleventh century, even the now prescribed lights and the no less obligatory crucifix did not formerly stand on the altar. At the Celebration of the Eucharist nothing was on the table save the cloths, the sacred vessels, the paten, and the Mass book. Hence there was nothing to distract the eyes of the faithful from the essential purpose, namely, the offering of the Holy Sacrifice, nothing to hinder the free view of the congregation in following the action. This took place freely and unconcealed before the eyes of all.

Liturgists have long asked when the decisive change came about which led to the present arrangements outside Rome, when the Priest was transferred from the back to the front of the altar, when the altar itself was put against the wall of the apse, when the retable was introduced, and lastly when a cross and a line of

candles were placed on the table. For some years we
have been sufficiently well informed about all this by
the remarkably learned investigations of Joseph
Braun. We now know that Celebration with the
priest's face averted from the congregation became
the general rule outside Rome *c.* A.D. 1000. The setting
of the altar on the far wall and the introduction of
retables followed soon afterwards. On the other hand
candles were not placed on the altar before *c.* 1100
and the Cross for the most part only when the age of
the Mysticism of the Passion began, i.e. in the
thirteenth century.

From all this it follows that the new additions to
the altar probably came in at almost the very period
when the Mass was beginning to be regarded as a
more or less exclusively priestly action. And it is also
certain that these changes in relation to the altar
essentially furthered that change in the people's
interpretation of the rite which we must in the main
deplore. Happily, in recent decades understanding of
the special function of the altar has grown everywhere.
In new churches, the altar is again given the dominant
place which belongs to it by right. Its character as a
table is stressed and it is disencumbered of the often
very trivial and distracting decoration of attached
structures and lace hangings. Perhaps we may hope
that a return to the original orientation of the altar
and the setting of it in the open and as a result the
disappearance of the unfortunate turnings of the priest
at *Dominus Vobiscum*, etc., will be the final stage of
this new development.

4. A third point which I wish to single out from the results of recent study concerns the Offertory Procession. In early times it was the universal practice at every Eucharist for the faithful to place a sacrificial gift on the altar or to deliver it at the altar rails. These were sometimes gifts which could be used either in making ready the Eucharist or on other occasions in divine service (bread, wine, oil, wax), sometimes gifts which were considered only as contributions to the support of the clergy or to the community's works of charity. But all were conceived and recognized as the symbolical expression of participation in the Sacrificial Action; and in this way the charitable activities of the community were given their roots in the central act of worship. Synods stressed the duty of taking part in this so-called Offertory Procession right down to the eleventh century, but from then on the admonitions of the Bishops cease. When the meaning of the Offertory ceremony had ceased to be understood and it had come to be regarded as only a concern of the Priest, the Offertory Procession also lost its rationale. All that has survived is the monetary alms, given, on the occasion of the Eucharist, for the poor or the needs of the Church. It is no longer brought in special processions to the altar. A minor church official collects the gifts of the congregation in a plate or alms-bag, while the priest at the altar takes no notice of the performance, but proceeds with the service without pause. More recent studies, which need, however, to be carried further, have shown that this stage was reached round about 1200. Only the

Consecration of a Bishop and the analogously constructed Dedication of an Abbot have retained, in the reduced form of the Offertory Procession of the candidate, this solemn procession.

It is the more remarkable that at the end of the fourteenth century, as I was able to show in the *Festschift* for Abbot Herwegen, the Offertory Procession, without any direct connexion with primitive practice but with all the colour which it must have had in the early Christian period, came to life again in the framework of the Solemnity of Canonization. What was the purpose of the Offertory Procession in the hands of those who drew up this rite at the Papal Court? Did they wish merely to give greater splendour to the service of Canonization? Or were they interested in the symbolism which could be connected with the proffered gifts? Or did they perhaps feel the need, by way of the rite of Canonization, of again securing general admission for an element of the early Christian Liturgy which elsewhere had been almost lost but which they regarded as valuable? We must leave such questions provisionally unanswered.

5. The last point that I wish to mention relates to Genuflexion. In antiquity, dropping the knee was both an expression of the sense of guilt and an attitude of petition, but it was also especially a symbol of worship. In this last sense it was practised in saluting a statue of a god, of a ruler regarded as a god, and of his portrait. It was for this reason that Christians in the Age of Persecution were compelled to refuse bending of the knee, as well as sacrifice, to the Imperial

portrait; for they could not adore his likeness. But by the middle of the third century this gesture was already so colourless and devoid of meaning that in wide circles of the Roman populace it was no longer conceived as a sign of worship. Hence in 275 the Roman state could officially declare that genuflexion belonged not to the elements of the pagan religion but to the outward forms of expression of civil loyalty, to the *Romanae caeremoniae*. But it was not until Constantine that the Church dared to draw the practical consequences of this new situation. From then on, the Church no longer scrupled at permitting the Emperor and his portrait to be honoured with the knee. It even encouraged the faithful to mark with the same respectful gesture such holy, but not worshipful, objects as the altar, relics, and pictures of the saints. Indeed, in the end it permitted that the Imperial privilege of being saluted with the bending of the knee should be accorded to Bishops. Henceforward in the Liturgy of the West genuflexion was not merely a gesture of penitence and prayer, but it became an established token of honour to the altar, relics of the Cross, crucifix and Bishop.

In the eleventh century, however, the liturgical genuflexion suddenly came to assume, in addition to its other and earlier meanings, the character of a gesture of worship. This came about when Berengar of Tours denied any conversion in the Eucharist. The Church then found herself obliged to stress with greater emphasis than hitherto the Presence of the God-man beneath the consecrated species. Hence, as

Peter Browe has succeeded in showing, there arose the practice of honouring the Eucharist by an act of genuflexion before its reception. This genuflexion before the God-man, Who was believed to be present, necessarily became a symbol of adoration. In consequence the gesture here won back in a Christian context a meaning which it had already lost in the pagan era. From now on the bending of the knee appears in a threefold rôle in the Liturgy. In Eucharistic worship it is a sign of adoration, whereas everywhere else it continues as before to be either a symbol of mere respect or a mark of penitence and prayer.

These facts create no small obstacle to the proper instruction of the faithful. It is difficult indeed to make it clear to a congregation which the worship of the Eucharist, which stands so prominently in the foreground, has accustomed from youth upwards to see in genuflexion a symbol of humiliation before God and of worship, that the bending of the knee before the altar in the absence of the tabernacle, and especially before the Bishop, is to be understood in a different sense. Might it not be well to take proper account of the change in meaning which this gesture assumed in the eleventh century and to permit the untabernacled altar and the Bishop to be honoured simply by a bow?

# IV

# THE EPOCH OF CHANGELESSNESS
## OR RUBRICISM

FROM THE COUNCIL OF TRENT TO THE PRESENT DAY

1. The fourth and last section of the history of the Roman Liturgy covers the period from the Council of Trent to the present time. Earlier students were accustomed to describe it somewhat as follows: The Liturgy, which was officially codified as a result of the Council (*Breviarium Romanum*, publd. 1568; *Missale Romanum*, 1570), was introduced step by step into every country, and without any great upheaval. The last to receive it were the Bishoprics of North-West Germany and of France in the course of the nineteenth century. The supreme Roman authority for liturgical matters, viz. the Congregation of Rites, which was created in 1588, secured by its authoritative interpretation of the liturgical rulings and its watchfulness over practice in every corner of the Church, that the codified Liturgy was performed with uniformity. Since the era of codification the rubricist, that is, the expert in liturgical law, has thus come to play a leading rôle in liturgical life—a circumstance which gives to this whole period its most marked characteristics. In this final period the spiritual life is determined only to a strictly limited extent by the Liturgy. It is conditioned to a correspondingly greater degree by devotion

to the Eucharistic Christ and His Sacred Heart, by the cult of Our Lady and by meditation. Some attempts made in the Age of the Enlightenment and in the Romantic Epoch to lead the faithful back to an intelligent participation in the Liturgy were without abiding or extended influence. It was only the renewal of strength in the Benedictine Order in the second half of the nineteenth century and above all the reforms of Pius X which inaugurated a general return to liturgical life.

More recent study has not shown the views of older scholars about the development of this liturgical period to be erroneous, except at a few points, though in many respects these conceptions have been widened or deepened. We will consider here a few specially important points.

2. Until recently it was assumed as a matter of course that the ceremonial current to-day in the veneration of the Sacrament of the Altar, which orders such things as the setting of the monstrance on a 'throne', the use of the baldacchino in processions of the Blessed Sacrament, and a developed system of outward expressions of worship, arose in the Middle Ages as part of the rapid growth of the Eucharistic movement. This is true to the extent that here and there these customs were already in use in the Middle Ages. But in general it was not until the sixteenth century, i.e. only at the beginning of our last period, that they became established practices. And this happened, as Joseph Kramp was the first to recognize, especially under the influence of the consideration that

the Eucharistic Christ was the King of Kings and that
He is therefore entitled to the marks of respect ruling
in the Court ceremonial of the sixteenth century and
to Court pomp in general.

The background of these processes of thought,
which is presumably to be found in the characteristic
mentality of the Baroque Age, is still in need of
elucidation in its details. That the considerations just
mentioned are still living factors in Romance lands is
to be seen, for instance, in Italy, in the widespread
organization of the Paggi del Santissimo Sacramento,
boys who at functions of special solemnity are decked in
a white silk Spanish costume and even provided with a
small dagger and stand around the altar. This, as our
readers will recall, is the second time in the history of
the Roman Liturgy when recourse has been had to the
etiquette of the secular Court. But while on the
former instance it was a case of giving distinction to
Bishops and clerics, it is here a question of the honour
due to the Lord Himself in His Eucharistic presence.

3. For a more precise knowledge of the historical
development of devotion to the Sacrament and of the
*Missa coram exposito Sanctissimo Sacramento* which grew
up with it we are indebted to Peter Browe. As Browe
(who had an impressive supporter in the French
scholar, Dumoutet) decisively proved, these new
forms of Eucharistic piety go back in the last resort
to the circumstance that since the end of the Middle
Ages the mere seeing of the Host exercised, to an ever
greater degree, a strong attraction on the faithful, on
the ground that a special power of benediction was

ascribed to the sight of it. The original champions of these new forms of devotion were pre-eminently the German dioceses. Indeed, one of the sixteenth-century Popes expressly refers to Exposition as a German custom. In the era of the Counter Reformation, it was especially the Jesuits who fostered the new devotional forms and by means of them doubtless exercised a deep influence on the faithful. On the other hand the Roman curia down to the last moment showed great reserve, especially in the matter of *Missae coram exposito*, and once again gave new evidence of its traditional glory and reputation, namely, to be extremely conservative in all that concerns the Liturgy. Moreover, at least as far as the *Missae coram exposito* were concerned, the curia showed at the same time a more penetrating insight into the essence of liturgical rites than the innovators. For who to-day would seriously talk of coupling the Sacrifice of the Eucharist with devotion to the Christ throned in the monstrance?

4. A few years ago, when examining the newly promulgated calendar of 1568 and 1570, put out by the Tridentine Commission, my seminar came on the track of a noteworthy fact. Two of its members, Ernst Focke (who fell in Russia) and Hans Heinrichs, who carried the subject further, published their results in an essay printed in 1939. This essay contained decisive proof that the Tridentine Commission on Liturgy acted in the most peremptory fashion in its reform of the calendar when it removed the feasts which the Church Year had incorporated in earlier centuries. Its method was to retain in the calendar

feasts which were celebrated in Rome itself down to the eleventh century, but to show grace only to a very small number of those which had been introduced later; and among the latter not a single German feast was retained.

Two important facts are here made clear. The first is that 'Roman Liturgy' still remains identical, both for the members of the Commission working on behalf of the Council of Trent and for others, with the Liturgy of the City of Rome, with its connexions with the local Roman saints and the local Roman churches. The Commission therefore believed that this character must be restored to the calendar, in so far as it had been lost. The other point is the belief that the early centuries are the ideal age of liturgical development, and that what came later is to a great extent an over-growth, which can and must be cast away.

The former of these ideas will probably no longer be defended in its full extent by the ruling authority in the Church. The age of absolute unification in the matter of what is locally Roman has now gone by. The Saints of the different lands are coming to occupy an ever more prominent place in the Church Year. And local liturgical traditions in matters affecting the dispensing of the Sacraments can reckon to-day on very considerable sympathy.

But the second point mentioned as having found expression in the Tridentine Commission, namely the notion that from the standpoint of liturgy the early centuries stand on a higher level than those which followed them, is of fundamental significance. For many minds are widely exercised by the problem as to how far it is ever right to designate developments in the history of liturgy as false without coming into conflict with a basic point of doctrine, namely the dogma of the guidance of the Church by the Holy Ghost which *ipso facto* excludes all definite error. They ask whether the oft-repeated cry, 'Back to the beginnings! Back to the Liturgy of the Early Church!' has not already far transgressed permissible limits. In helping us to answer this acute problem, the practical standpoint of the Tridentine Commission makes a not inconsiderable contribution.

5. The occasional tensions between Roman legislation and local praxis have directed the attention of liturgists to a remarkable fact, namely that in some circumstances Rubricism, through the emphasis which its method lays on the circumstantial (*Zuständliche*), can lead an action or ordinance of the liturgy in a direction contrary to that of its original intention. It may even set it permanently in this new direction, unless, indeed, customary usages, directly opposed to it, do not, as is often the case, correct the decision of Rubricism. Two instances of the operation of this principle may be given.

Such mosaics as the glorious phalanx of Dalmatian saints at S. Venanzio at the Lateran in Rome still give us an impressive picture of what the chasuble and the dalmatic, the two most important liturgical robes, looked like in the early period of vestments. The chasuble, the liturgical garment of the Bishop and Priest (the Bishop's representative), was a bell-shaped

vesture which reached down to the feet, made of light-
weight material, usually of a dark colour, and gathered
up on both sides sufficiently to give the necessary
freedom of movement to the hands and lower arms.
By contrast the dalmatic, the liturgical vestment of
the Deacon and Subdeacon, was a very loosely-made
white tunic, with broad sleeves, in cut strikingly
similar to the cowl of the Benedictine monk of to-day.
In beauty and solemnity, these two types of vesture
probably cannot be surpassed. To me they are among
the classical creations of man and are valid for all time.
The chasuble with its essentially oval flowing folds
and its dark shade of colour emphasizes the dignity of
the priestly shepherd of the community, who has
grown to maturity with the years, while the dalmatic,
with its light colour, its simple vertical folds and its
sleeves made for freedom of action, effectively emphasizes the ministering character of the youthful assistant.
As has been made clear by the researches of Joseph
Braun, the chasuble and dalmatic, despite many
different changes in colour, material and decoration,
preserved in essentials their original forms through
the centuries, until the Baroque Age, here as everywhere in its remarkable self-sufficiency sweeping
everything aside, fundamentally changed the structure
of both vestments. Down to that time they were real
articles of clothing: they then became ornaments, that
is, decorative and stiff pieces of embellishment, which
hung down like scapulas over the breast and back. As
the degenerate Baroque type of chasuble and dalmatic
was the form of the vesture in the age of liturgical

codification and also the style which harmonized with the majority of the churches in Rome, rubricism peremptorily laid it down as authoritative. Thus it came about that such a decree as that issued by the Congregation of Rites on December 9, 1925, was possible, ordering that 'Gothic Chasubles'—for so the traditional pre-Baroque form of the chasuble was erroneously termed—were essentially inadmissible.

We will now give our second instance. From very early times the first part of the Eucharistic prayer ended with a reference to the heavenly worship of God by the Angels. At this point in the service the faithful at Rome, from the third century onwards, interrupted the solemn worship of the Celebrant by coming in with the Sanctus, the Song of the Angels in the Old Testament which was already in use in the Liturgy of the Synagogue. The Bishop or Priest waited for this chant to end and not until it was finished did he continue the recitation (in a loud voice, as we have already learnt) of the Canon. But the awareness that both parts of the Canon, now separated by the Sanctus, belonged together was gradually lost. As a result the second part of the Eucharistic prayer was no longer sung by the Celebrant, but only spoken. Eventually, as we have already remarked, the audible recitation of the second and more important part of the Canon was given up. Many would now find it meaningless to allow the Celebrant to remain waiting for the Sanctus to end. And the delay became increasingly tedious, especially as from an early date the singing of the Sanctus had been given over by the people to the choir and had developed into a long piece of formal music. The result was to convert the Sanctus into a hymn which bridged the silence between the Preface and Consecration. When the polyphonic music of the Baroque era led to even further elaboration of the Sanctus, the practice was introduced of not singing the second part of the hymn, viz. the Benedictus, until after the Consecration, especially as the text of the Sanctus seemed to justify this division. Hence there came the formal ruling of the Sacred Congregation of Rites which forbade the singing of the Benedictus before the Consecration (*S.R.C.*, January 14, 1921).

It would seem that Pius XI wisely recognized the danger which would threaten a rational and organic development of the Western Liturgy if its destinies were left solely in the hands of rubricists. On February 6, 1930, he created a historical department of the Congregation of Rites which was to be consulted in all liturgical questions. We may be allowed to hope that in future this newly constituted body will succeed in preventing decisions which, such as that just mentioned, fail to do justice to the historic meaning of liturgical rites and ordinances.

\*　　\*　　\*

Those who have read and pondered on these pages will be unable to avoid the impression that the smallest alteration or novelty in the realm of liturgy may be compared with an avalanche. The beginning of the change may be wholly unnoticed and yet it can lead to infinitely far-reaching results. We need only reflect on how much that was unlooked for came about when the Canon was first prayed silently. Indeed, we may say that out of this small deviation from traditional practice the whole development of Christian devotion in later centuries derives, with all the limitations which we with our deeper insight to-day deplore.

The reader who has convinced himself from this single example of the great responsibility which rests on those who take a decisive step in this field will cease to be impatient when faced with all the practical questions aroused by the problem of liturgical renewal. Many decades of intensive constructive thought and consideration are not too long when the task is that of giving shape to the further development of a living organism which can look forward to a long and purposeful history in the ages to come.

# BIBLIOGRAPHY

*[It is hoped that the following list, which includes most of the items referred to by Professor Klauser in his text, may be of service to students.—F. L. C.]*

A. ALFÖLDI, 'Die Ausgestaltung des monarchischen Zeremoniells am römischen Kaiserhofe' in *Mitteilungen des Deutschen Archäologischen Instituts*. Römische Abteilung, xlix (1934), pp. 1–118.

A. ALFÖLDI, 'Insignien und Tracht der römischen Kaiser', ibid., l (1935), pp. 1–171.

M. ANDRIEU, *Les* Ordines Romani *du haut Moyen-Âge*. I, Les Manuscrits. II, Les Textes (Ordines I–XIII). III, Les Textes (Ordines XIV–XXXIV). Spicilegium Sacrum Lovaniense 11 (1931), 23 (1948) and 24 (1951).

A. BAUMSTARK, *Vom Geschichtlichen Werden der Liturgie*. Ecclesia Orans X (1923).

A. BAUMSTARK, 'Ein Übersetzungsfehler im Messkanon' in *Studia Catholica* v (1929), pp. 378–382.

A. BAUMSTARK, *Liturgie Comparée*. Conférences faites au Prieuré d'Amay. Édition refondue (1940).

E. BISHOP, 'The Genius of the Roman Rite' in *Weekly Register*, May 1899, reprinted in *Liturgica Historica* (1918), pp. 1–19.

E. BISHOP—A. WILMART, O.S.B., *Le Génie du Rit Romain* (Paris, 1920). [Fr. transl. of preceding item, with additions.]

B. BOTTE, O.S.B., *Le Canon de la Messe Romaine*. Édition critique, introduction et notes (1935).

J. BRAUN, S.J., *Die liturgische Gewandung im Occident und Orient nach Ursprung und Entwicklung, Verwendung und Symbolik* (1907).

J. BRAUN, S.J., *Der christliche Altar in seiner geschichtlichen Entwicklung* (2 vols., 1924).

J. BRAUN, S.J., *Das christliche Altargerät in seinem Sein und in seiner Entwicklung* (1932).

P. BROWE, S.J., *Die Verehrung der Eucharistie im Mittelalter* (1933).

P. BROWE, S.J., *Die häufige Kommunion im Mittelalter* (1938).

P. BROWE, S.J., *Die eucharistischen Wunder des Mittelalters.* Breslauer Studien zur historischen Theologie. Neue Folge, Band iv (1938).

P. BROWE, S.J., *Die Pflichtkommunion im Mittelalter* (1940).

B. CAPELLE, O.S.B., 'Le Pape Gélase et la Messe romaine' in *Revue d' Histoire Ecclésiastique*, xxxv (1939), pp. 22–34.

O. CASEL, O.S.B., 'Oblatio rationabilis' in *Theologische Quartalschrift*, xcix (1917–18), pp. 429–38.

O. CASEL, O.S.B., *Das Gedächtnis des Herrn in der altchristlichen Liturgie.* Ecclesia Orans II (1918).

O. CASEL, O.S.B., *De Philosophorum Graecorum Silentio Mystico* (1919).

O. CASEL, O.S.B., 'Das Mysteriengedächtnis der Messliturgie im Lichte der Tradition' in *Jahrbuch für Liturgiewissenschaft*, vi (1926), pp. 113–204.

O. CASEL, O.S.B., 'Art und Sinn der ältesten christlichen Osterfeier' in *Jahrbuch für Liturgiewissenschaft*, xiv (1938), pp. 1–78.

O. CASEL, O.S.B., 'Glaube, Gnosis und Mysterium' in *Jahrbuch für Liturgiewissenschaft*, xv (1941), pp. 155–305.

R. H. CONNOLLY, O.S.B., *The so-called Egyptian Church Order and Derived Documents.* Cambridge Texts and Studies, VIII, No. 4 (1916).

E. DUMOUTET, *Le Désir de Voir l' Hostie et les Origines de la Dévotion au Saint-Sacrement* (1926).

E. FOCKE and H. HEINRICHS, 'Das Kalendarium des *Missale Pianum* und seine Tendenzen' in *Theologische Quartalschrift*, cxx (1939), pp. 383–400 and 461–69.

## BIBLIOGRAPHY

R. GUARDINI, *The Spirit of the Liturgy*. Eng. tr. by A. Lane (1930).

H. HEINRICHS. [*See* E. FOCKE.]

J. A. JUNGMANN, S.J., *Die Stellung Christi im liturgischen Gebet*. Liturgiegeschichtliche Forschungen, vii–viii (1925).

T. KLAUSER, 'Die Liturgie der Heiligsprechung' in *Heilige Überlieferung*. Ausschnitte aus der Geschichte des Mönchtums und des heiligen Kultes, dem hochwürdigsten Herrn Abte von Maria Laach . . . Ildefons Herwegen zum silbernen Abtsjubiläum, herausgeg. O. Casel, O.S.B. (1938), pp. 212 33.

T. KLAUSER, 'Der Übergang der römischen Kirche von der griechischen zur lateinischen Liturgiesprache' in Miscellanea Giovanni Mercati, *Studi e Testi*, cxxi (1946), pp. 467–82.

J. KRAMP, S.J., 'Messgebräuche der Gläubigen in der Neuzeit' in *Stimmen der Zeit*, cxi (1926), pp. 206–23.

J. KRAMP, S.J., 'Messgebräuche der Gläubigen in den ausserdeutschen Ländern' in *Stimmen der Zeit*, cxiii (1927), pp. 352–67.

H. LIETZMANN, *Messe und Herrenmahl*, Eine Studie zur Geschichte der Liturgie. Arbeiten zur Kirchengeschichte VIII (1926).

E. SCHWARTZ, *Über die pseudoapostolischen Kirchenordnungen*. Schriften der wissenschaftlichen Gesellschaft in Strassburg, vi (1910).

G. SÖHNGEN, *Symbol und Wirklichkeit im Kultmysterium* (ed. 2, 1940).

G. SÖHNGEN, *Das sakramentale Wesen des Messopfers* (1946).

## A Selection of Professor Klauser's Publications

*Die Cathedra im Totenkult der heidnischen und christlichen Antike.* Liturgiegeschichtliche Forschungen, Heft ix (1927).

'Ein vollständiges Evangelienverzeichnis der römischen Kirche aus dem 7 Jahrhundert, erhalten im Cod. Vat. Pal. lat. 46' in *Römische Quartalschrift* xxxv (1927), pp. 113–34.

'Eine Stationsliste der Metzer Kirche aus dem 8. Jahrhundert, wahrscheinlich ein Werk Chrodegangs' in *Ephemerides Liturgicae* xliv (1930), pp. 162–93.

'Die liturgischen Austauschbeziehungen zwischen der römischen und der fränkisch-deutschen Kirche vom 8. bis zum 11. Jahrhundert' in *Historisches Jahrbuch*, liii (1933), pp. 169–89.

*Das römische Capitulare evangeliorum.* Texte und Untersuchungen zu seiner ältesten Geschichte (I: Typen). Liturgiegeschichtliche Quellen und Forschungen, Heft xxviii (1935).

'Die konstantinischen Altäre der Lateranbasilika' in *Römische Quartalschrift*, xliii (1935), pp. 179–86.

*Taufet in lebendigem Wasser.* Zum religions- und kulturgeschichtlichen Verständnis von Didache, 7, 1–3. *Pisciculi Franz Joseph Dölger dargeboten* (1939), pp. 157–64.

*Doctrina Duodecim Apostolorum, Barnabae Epistula.* Florilegium Patristicum, fasc. i (new ed., 1940).

*Der Ursprung der bischöflichen Insignien und Ehrenrechte.* Rede gehalten beim Antritt des Rektorats der Rheinischen Friedrich-Wilhelms-Universität zu Bonn am 11. Dezember 1948. Bonner Akademische Reden, I. [1949.]

Prof. Klauser is also the editor of the *Reallexikon für Antike und Christentum* (1942, ff.) to which he has contributed, *inter alia*, the artt. 'Abraham' and 'Akklamation'.

See also p. 61 s.v. T. Klauser.

# INDEX